THE WILLING EYE

Tracy Ryan was born in 1964 in Western Australia, where she grew up. After reading English at Curtin University, she studied European languages at the University of Western Australia, and has translated many French writers, including Hélène Cixous, Maryline Desbiolles and Françoise Hàn. She now lives in Cambridge, where she has worked as a bookseller, tutor, editor and writer. She was Judith E. Wilson Junior Visiting Fellow at Robinson College, Cambridge, in 1998, and recently taught Australian literature and film at the University of East Anglia. Her books include two collections, *Killing Delilah* (1994) and *Bluebeard in Drag* (1996), and a novel, *Vamp* (1997), all published in Australia by Fremantle Arts Centre Press. *The Willing Eye* is her third book-length collection, and her first to be published in Britain.

TRACY RYAN

The Willing Eye

BLOODAXE BOOKS

ISBN: 1 85224 506 9

This edition published 1999 by
Bloodaxe Books Ltd,
P.O. Box 1SN,
Newcastle upon Tyne NE99 1SN.

First published in Australia in 1999 by
Fremantle Arts Centre Press.

Bloodaxe Books Ltd acknowledges
the financial assistance of Northern Arts.

Cover printing by J. Thomson Colour Printers Ltd, Glasgow.

Printed in Great Britain by
Cromwell Press Ltd, Trowbridge, Wiltshire.

for Katherine

Acknowledgements

Acknowledgements are due to the editors of the following publications where some of these poems first appeared: *The Adelaide Review*, *Arena*, *Cordite*, *Kunapipi*, *Landbridge: Contemporary Australian Poetry* (FACP/Arc, 1999), *New Blood* (Bloodaxe Books, 1999), *Poetry* (Chicago), *Salt*, *Scarp*, *Subvoicive*, *The Times Literary Supplement*, *La Traductière*, *Ulitarra*, *Varuna New Poetry*, *Wasafiri* and *Westerly*.

Tracy Ryan wishes to thank the Australia Council for giving her a Category B Writer's Grant to help her work on this book.

Contents

BREATH

Enough

You sleep on one side, your spine
the spine of a closed book,
your immaculate symmetry
folded in on itself,
the inside mysterious as
a Rorschach blot.
But the nurse laughs at aesthetics,
says our doubling
is designed for survival, the world
being full of people who walk about
with one lung, for instance,
labouring under the weight
of absence yet looking no different
from the rest of us. And yes,
if death or something more necessary should
sever us, I'd continue just
like that – taking in, I imagine,
only half the air but still enough.

Spin

Holding us all at once, I watch
this green world over your shoulder while
my daughter, wedged between us, can only
see sideways, the price of flying
over these soft contour banks that look
safe but would nonetheless crack
any bones we offered.
Unhelmeted, we ride
the borders of oatfields
yielding to wind like the tread of some
spectre I cannot follow,
my feet thrust in the bike's flanks
as if in stirrups
for a difficult birth. I believe
these roads know you just as
my body at night knows your body
will never hurt me. Your faith
inspires: breathes in & restores, even as
that wind tries
to distort our words.

Breath

in the pooling dark a sonar
connection

or a musical notation
only a mother can read

just as my lungs
sang her out, now

I listen her
into sleep

help her drop
over that voiceless edge

& yet
survive;

first faster when
the eyelids flicker

as if I could simply lift
them & look in on

her psyche, so close
to the surface

then slower, lowering
into dreams as a

weary body sinks
in a warm bath – a shudder, sigh,

& I can
safely leave the room.

Ballet Class

Crammed into an ante-room, parents
wait out the half-hour,
some reading papers, but more
tracking anxiously through the curtains
this stretching & shuffling,
willing grace into little limbs like
a gift at a christening
the Good Fairy Dance
the Bad Fairy Dance
but the toddlers glance back
at Mum or Dad & don't take
notice of the mirrors.
One boy in black
looks lost among the mini-tutus.
Katherine squats in a corner
rejecting what she nagged all year for.

Flute Lessons

1

My old schoolfriend Margaret
having read my book
writes from Byron Bay
Thought it must be you;
do you still
play the flute?

We were thirteen, she taught me
so fast, that August
in her room, that the school would report
the most amazing progress
seen to date.

We grew apart.
She took up smoking, went
after boys, I toyed
with classical guitar,

haven't touched the flute
in fifteen years. What note
does she hear
to be so sure
I am one & the same?

2

You can't
chew gum or eat sweets before
you play: it coats
the inside of the instrument
once sullied, never regained

& this notch
that proves perfect pitch
we check like a hymen

with a soft cloth we chasten
the silver
of our fingerprints

we are dedicated as saints
aiming for firsts
in the orchestra

Margaret gets there
my long notes
need practice.

3
In our household
all of the kids learned woodwind
except the brother who later died.
We shared the instruments:
some played reeds but I
trusted my own mouth better.
Margaret taught me the embouchure.
Our teacher's cheeks were deeply scored
with twenty years of it
as if he were smiling regardless of mood,
another pied piper.
We stood at the mirror
as others did with lipstick;
practised at every spare moment
much as I was later taught
to flex the pelvic floor
ready for childbirth.

4
I lie on the floor
trying to find my belly

The teacher says
my scales are perfect but
my long notes like
rough drafts

I plead asthma
it doesn't wash

I must forget
how we breathe
when we stand upright

I must lie
corpse-like
learn to inhale
to sustain
& expel.

Non-swimmer

Four summers & still
merely working on confidence,
she will not float or venture
far from the steps
though she loves to watch
her uncle make deep laps –
lungful & muscle resisting
the urge to burst upward,
draped in water.
Not until her smaller cousin
leaps in, fearless,
does she suddenly immerse her face,
lifting it dripping, a new print.

Edge

On the first day I warned her
making her say it back like
name & address,

on that day a boy
went right through the ice
over an edge that dipped
to let him off
like the step on the school bus.

We who didn't know him
collected our children,
our talk sealed but
thin in patches.

Walking home
I told her nothing –
it took all our effort
to keep from slipping

on glittering earth so prone
to partial disclosure,
stony as ever under
the great white lie
that snow is.

Stork Picture

My daughter makes a stork picture.
She wants it to be in Australia.
But I tell her as far as I know
We have no storks there
Bringing the dead souls
Into newborn bodies.

Her stork is facing
A quaint house, like the dollhouse
I had in childhood
Whose front swung open
Like the one in the Mansfield story –
'That is the way for a house to open!'
Nothing is hidden.

Her house has curtains
And window-boxes
And looks European
Though she insists now it's African
Because that's where the storks go
When winter comes.

She asks why they build their nests
On the homes of humans.
I can't answer that one.

We put up the picture as some
Put up platforms
To persuade the storks to come
And crown their houses.

Tonight she'll dream
Of a roof with broad, warm wings
Folded in.

The Splinter

Unable to sleep though the day's
been long, she feels the weight
as the princess felt the pea.

I spread her palm to read
for likelihood
of wheedling out

as I've often done
from her skin and my own
that art of persuasion

as if I were selling something:
the treat to follow or
the solace
of bread to bite down on,

the game of breathing
I learnt from birth-pain
she doesn't remember.

But it's in too far, this sliver
finer than finger
or tweezer can call back.

Fearful, she pictures
the layers closing over,
soft dough with foreign body
baked dangerously in.

Tomorrow I'll buy a needle,
recall my own mother running
pin-tip through flame,
the silver clouded
to rainbowed black,

then chasing the thing but finding
only nerve-endings
hooking out knots of blood like the useless
French stitches we learnt at school.

Holding this memory up
like a map, I will enter
the merest surface
of her little hand to find
the random invader,

no blind stabbing this time but
small pain with purpose
of preventing greater,
reassure her
our bodies are solid but open
at every pore.

Indenture

Late enough now for doing
secret duty, as at Christmas.
I tiptoe in for the glass
in which a shed tooth
lies like something sunken:
toy treasure in a fishbowl,
capsule refusing
dissolution.

Sharp between fingers as
it was on that first biting
of my breast, emblem
of readiness for the next thing:
how growth brings distance,
contact proves separation.

Oddly dislodged and rootless,
unbloodied –
what can be done with it
and still keep faith?
Taken and paid for,
wrapped like the usual garbage,
without rehearsal,
unsentimental.

Acts of Faith

1

When my daughter edged down,
crimson berry, fruit of my
womb, that head thrusting out, then
retracting, as a balloon
will fail until just
enough breath is forced in,
I could hold nothing
back. The coach urged:

Zero station, station plus one, imagine
you are a camera on full aperture
you are a flower, imagine
your whole body opening
like time-lapse pictures.

Imagine that. All this science
& all I could say: *Let it be done, let it be*
done to me according to your word.

2

Likewise you ease in
bit by bit, draw out
& try again, folding
fingers, a cat
retracting claws. My walls
resist – I tell them
birth in reverse, those images
that prevented tearing. Soon
you murmur *I'm right in there*
& I hardly believe my body's
trust, your fist fits
perfectly, as a mystery fits
an unasked question. I open,
I open, my edges raw but soft
like pages cut for the first time.

BITE

Hot Sex

Burning my lips' edge
Like echoes of rough play
Or the way childbirth
Forced me to walk bent
With cunt like torn metal
Forgetful
Of all else: your fingers
Inside me, after chopping
Chillies for dinner.

Portrait with Glasses

Losing them once
in the ocean
you had to be led back to shore
like someone steered earthward
after a baptism

though they translate
my world into yours &
back again
I cannot see through them

always a little bit broken
you fear for them
clear eggshells I
might walk on

left at the bedside
while lovemaking
the first thing you feel for
in the morning

Bite

Dark corsage I can't
unpin, I'm stuck with it,
drawing wry comment
for days, however I hide
this stamp that approves
the boundary, proves that you
stop short of blood, all jokes
aside. But note
how readily my veins
leap up: a little harder and
the whole heart would follow,
I'd turn inside out, bleak pocket
for your rummaging,
magician's hat. And yet
I don't; I let you pass
like this small stormcloud on
my white, impassive throat.

Smoking the Butts

We are down to this, as if all the small
defences against loss
must be unrolled and tried again, like
those bong-strainings you work up
in the kitchen,
like a lover you meant to drop.

I am not allowed to
throw them away; they pile up like
ammunition. Out on the street,
you swerve and dip for them, pigeon
after anyone's crumbs. Whose breath,
whose spit, not your concern – each
wrinkled bit a talisman getting you through
the lean times, the fear   the fear
we are down to this, there may be nothing left
between us.

Curse

It was promised
at your christening
I wasn't around then

all the spindles were
duly hidden but you sought
them out

sure as gravity you drop
like blood does

my kiss is useless

everything stops at the age
you were

26

Washday

Distorted and self-conscious, these flannel
shirts, bruised Levis, not quite perished,
strung out as if for examination
of conscience,

they want
at least another cycle, still smell
of the Globe Hotel, the empty flat, the limestone
grit of that last cave, the lives
before this one

woven now into the fabric
that will never soften.

You say you know the right
way to peg them but insist
on any old way,
warn me against rehanging.

Lentils

Dispiriting, a string of spilt
beads, they lie,
pebbles from a cold French beach
under water already clouding.

Everything thrown in
will take on
their powdery sea-green
soft and spreading like mould on
old bread,

this food of
lean times, making do
without you –
the days between the visions
eked out with grey
small change.

I will colour them
with cummin, coriander
and cardamom – anything
to help them slip down
thick as the wet dirt eaten
at Lourdes by Bernadette:
what others count
an act of folly, my act of faith.

EXCURSIONS

Canning Bridge

Appearing less to link two banks than
brace itself against them
like fact or fate against two fools, this feat we travel
daily, willing the distance shorter. We marvel
at a river so forceful all manmade
structures seem to stride upstream and fight it.
Et nos amours... You on the west side
tell me the well-intentioned
have stripped all barnacles, created
algal bloom where they only meant
to clean things up. Here on the east
I wade in clear silt soft as our bodies but
emerge with filthy skin and disillusion:
hope must indeed be violent in
face of such interference and
contamination: *comme la vie est lente*...

Mt Henry Bridge

Clock-like, our steps
measure the bridge's underbelly
and back, rehearsing distance
and reconnaissance, across
a river so unequivocally black it looks
like heaven has fallen, or we've ascended.
A gull loops low, fluorescent,
over the water's imperceptible surface.
You joke and offer your good hand, not
your hook. But down on the bank,
fish leap to your shadow, acknowledge
old treaties – that once-red scrawl has
long since sunk into the

bridge wall – PROPERTY OF
no longer relevant, all quarrels now
absorbed or resolved, unlike small boys
on the far bank who dangle
avid rods and brag of *schnookie*
so big they'd drag you under
if you had no foothold. You walk now
by faith in the half-light and I follow,
your face silver as moon above
or below me.

Canning Dam

Against such mass
and vacancy, even the tallest
figure dwindles
to black speck on frosty concrete,
vanishes into the dry abyss.
Waiting,
I recall mountains
above Göschenen
these same colours,
how the breath rushed from me
and I wished the snow
would cover us. The dam
is low now, red gravel thickly rings
what water's there, and the rampart's
closed for inspection or repair. Small chance
of your courted flood today, but I still hold
breath for both of us until
you loom large at last and scale
the spillway wall.

Portrait or Landscape

It's a matter of angle
& degree, which bits you choose
to throw into relief or minimise

whether you focus
on fool or precipice

like the brother who used you in photos
only for scale

or merely turning the paper, try
to convey the whole terrain
that swallows all figures

aim for that broad & flat
detachment others call vision.

Wungong

I always dream he is down here
where he waved one hand and sank
in the still pool. I forget the real
dank fistful of dirt and agapanthus
we threw on him, I forget
red clods that adhered to
our soles and dust smeared
on damp cheeks, the unjust softness
of kangaroo paws. I forget HE IS RISEN
clamped over the earth-mouth.
In dreams I come back for him
to the one dam you have never
written of.

Quarry

It's these edges we covet
as if seeking the ridge that
betrays a trapdoor or
the hem of a blanket we'd
crawl in under. But edges are
eaten by water and never
the same place twice,
or left like this quarry to grow
slowly unstable: DANGER – FRAGILE
CLIFFS just waiting for
two fools to hold hands and drive
blindly over.

Pinjarra

Not healing but something
altogether more violent, like
the slap that engenders breath or
the blow that thwarts choking, this,
your more truly arrival or intervention than
presence in the landscape, damp once
under my child-feet in pursuit
of a mother I thought would drown herself,
site where histories bigger than ours compete,
where I learnt at school of the
slaughter of whites but was never told
the rest. We negotiate bank
and jetty, pick over stories like the names
of native birds or plants, find points
of entry in each other. I never thought
the land could resume being flat,
colours merely present themselves
to the eye without sting or saturation.
Even the graveyard today fails to be Gothic.
I walk in your more certain steps
these slopes that test memory like muscle
find it can flex after all and fall
painlessly back into place.

Penguin Island

By pure chance catching
the last boat of the last
day of the season

building on a connection others think
tenuous as this vanishing
sandbank where the sign warns
LIVES HAVE BEEN LOST

we cross and head for the summit
like making Stations
at each stop meditating

not on suffering but
on regeneration –

gulls' eggs fallen
from a high nest yet
intact, perfect
in abandonment,

on movement through
recuperating dunes and around
brooding penguins only the subtle ear
can sense

touching and leaving things as
we know we must
each other – as found.

Bluff Knoll

Thought not possible,
the elements so conspiring
only a fool would attempt
Bluff Knoll today – but two,
not even leaving names
with the ranger, or estimated
time of return, might well
between them make that veiled peak,
one reckless and seeking audience with
whatever awaits, and one content
to stumble in awe below this
cloud of unknowing. It's like
an arranged marriage you have to work
your way into, sensing yourself
develop flesh of the earth's flesh, bone
of the mountain's bone, inevitable
consummation. Past a certain point,
there's no return, even when you come down.

NEAR

May Day Fair at Reach

'Stinging things have a bad reputation;
they're lovely really.' – STALL ATTENDANT

These bees are less real than those we imagine
Or know from countless poems
Displaying the perfection of form
Afforded only by death-in-resin, or
The containment of these panes
Lifted for ghoulish inspection
Like a slice-of-life, in which the diverse mass
Dashes itself against glass.
Nowhere to hide from our light.
A woman shudders
But can't help looking. The kids
Want only knowledge of honey, the strict
Geometry of cells. They've shot,
Hooked, hammered, pitched and pinned
All afternoon, with little to show for it
But sacs of goldfish the cat will get tonight
Cheap toys as plush as the bees.
Four weeks at most, the keeper says
Bees last. On such a scale
And with such perverse insistence
On vanishing into the whole, on sacrifice,
Nothing seems too brutal, any notion
Outside utility unthinkable.

Beekeeper in Wandlebury Wood

zips in on a cycle like milkman
or butcher's boy

one zealous eye on us
the other on
his boxes sectioned
& severed like the trick
boxes of the magician

he can take out layers
& slide them in again
say there's no harm
done

teach us to watch
violence
without wincing

is it toughness
or indifference

around the hives
he pulls up nests of nettles,
bare-handed.

Near

Exploding slow and grey from the green
that is soon seen to be clouds of nettle,
little by little the stone
unpicks itself. We enter
its open spaces or leave
the world's enclosure.

However much mind tries
to reconstruct
logic and function, we feel
just like the children, adrift
in this maze whose centre
no longer is. Restless, they climb
despite our protests.
Their cries cauterise silence.

All's sealed in spite of lying
exposed to spring skies.
I push at absent walls
that won't admit, like leaning
on mirrors.

How quiet even the river is.
Skell, you ancient secret
of Trappist cleanliness
whose name means *resounding*
though that is forgotten now –
you with the nettles so plentiful
we can't get near.

Trompe l'œil

Look how the table's becoming
a table again,
as coach turns to pumpkin
only slower.

The marquetry's starting
to separate, making
rips in the fabric
of deception

just as my face takes rifts
under the same old daily
make-up, flesh begging
to differ.

It's as if the picture
were failing
through lack of someone's
faith

but who is it asking?
Who was that letter meant for
& what were the downturned cards
about to tell?

Our fingers want
to pick them up
but slip on glaze
rebarbative as mirrors,

itch over coins, quill, signet
& sealing wax.

Some kind of hoax.
Was it a joke only contemporaries
were meant to get,

an innocent talking point,
favourite set-piece?

Or did Boilly suspect we'd stand here
two centuries later
by his elaborate *memento mori*
still marvelling at his virtual skill,

the willing eye
a hopeless romantic that
can only be cheated?

The Birthday

Not one would mind, neither bird nor tree,
If mankind perished utterly;

And Spring herself, when she woke at dawn,
Would scarcely know that we were gone.
— SARA TEASDALE

Were beth they biforen us weren ...?
— ANON. 14TH-15TH C.

1

Tonight I sit after the party
to mark six years, unable to move
chairs back into place or shift
shed glitter from floor.

Six years of knowing nothing
and finding that out, spectator
of otherness
locked yet flimsy as that little
diary the best friend gave you.
Knowing I'll never touch it.

Already the body's
forgotten the milk-ache,
the melting,
how you lay each night in the crook
of my arm.

One of the guests, it seems,
gave birth on the same day.

Too long ago to swap notes
but she did say
Remember, it was the Gulf War.

2

Your still small body
really fallen into sleep
as only the utterly confident
can fall.

3

He says
You underestimate.
It is experience tells me this.
I have seen children
During the Blitz, you know?
(And I have no rejoinder.)
They are tough, tougher
Than any of us.
You must not
Keep things from her.

4

Luśka with the lovely voice
sings and dances out
her Spice Girls obsession
for the other children.

I tell the mothers
when I was eleven it
was the Bay City Rollers.

One day she'll tell
the same sort of anecdote
with the same pleasurable
embarrassment.
I can't of course
tell her that.

5

These things were trivial but
real. Elsewhere other things
went on. I am a nothing. However
as you preen in the sweet pink
fairy-suit, enjoying
your universe,
I can't tell you that. Who'd take
candy from a baby? What's this
need to protect and whom et cetera?
I'm glib enough
to pray for fine weather, for your day,
as if there were not
tragedies to think of.

                You pushed out
of me like a swimmer kicking
from the pool's edge
for momentum. That's who I am
and who you'll be. It is particular
to us, this knowledge, I don't care
what they say.

   6

Yesterday after a few things in the local
paper, we rehearsed the bit where
you don't get into anyone's car,
the lines they try about sweets, sick
mothers or needing directions.

Okay, you take it from there.

   7

If I let it all out it would crush you.
Who wants the Blitz?
Who are the adults
those children became?

I am a dam, a fortress for you
or stand at least
before you as lens to delicate
retina

anyway doing my best.

   8

Foolish to think these late
soft rains show any tenderness.

Yet to get on with this
I need to believe against

indifference, to touch something
remote as the hem of a garment

knowing I have no right
to be here, yet insisting

you must, I must, I am.

46

The Lesson
(an anti-pastoral)

The small schoolgirl
   on her way down
      grey Portugal Lane
       late for class
who brushes a careless
   hand against
     the one green
       nettle that had to sprout
     from yards of concrete
can't believe
   there's no dock leaf
         to cancel
       it out.

Noli Me Tangere

1

The Round Church, Church of the Holy
Sepulchre, of the Resurrection, is
not cross-shaped like most, but circular,
as early Christians circled
the tomb, the empty centre:
a pilgrim's ritual.

I imagine them all
in a ring
like the dreamt-of creature
biting its tail
that gave us the benzene molecule,
subconscious answer.

Or some picture by Escher
parading still.
Still they move round,
invisible, the blind
leading the blind
without falling,
their hope encoded, blunt
in Norman stone.

Later ages
added chambers,
carved in angels,
bolstered weakness.

Now the round nave
that stood alone
is less than half the structure.

To get the picture,
to walk the original circle,
you have to enter.

2

The latest modification
is that stained glass
gracing the East Window

whose theme, the brochure tells us
is hope, the Lamb-Who-Was-Slain.

This takes the place
of earlier glass
dislodged by a wartime bomb.

The brochure doesn't mention
what the theme was then.

3

At Holy Trinity the priest says
the first picture requested
out of protective storage
by the British public
after wartime danger
was Titian's *Noli me tangere*

which I've never noticed
in the National Gallery
though I've been there twice.

He talks of two
on the road to Emmaus
looking without seeing,
speaking without sense of
their own words.
          Of how
at the moment they recognised him
Christ left them, always
displaced, the word that was
on the tip of our tongues, the dream
dispersed upon waking, the poem
that will not be touched.

4

Their hearts burned within them
as the bulb burns with unseen light
when the earth warms
just enough for the green & then
the bloom to shoot up,
its loveliness shortlived
as moments of knowledge,
only half the truth. Truth is also
the nubbly corms in the cold earth
planted one year in Jarrahdale
where Easter comes long before spring,
pagan & Christian quite out of kilter,
forced into holes
scarcely wide enough, with a crowbar
in clay too hard for anything
but stubborn optimism. I assume
the flowers came up – by spring
the marriage was dead & I'd left there.
I hope somebody saw them.

5

Faith blows hot & cold
as Cambridge in spring
where late snow dissipates
before reaching any surface
where nothing penetrates

where those who drank in
yesterday's sun
are caught out now, ill-dressed
for this fickleness,

for this world whose seasons
no longer offer
stable metaphors for
spiritual states.

But then you were never
afraid of change
God of transitions
God of this Easter

constant & steadfast only
in your refusal
to be pinned there.

6

Why are you weeping?
Who is it you are looking for?

I speak to you here & always as
Mary spoke to the Gardener,
seeing only my loss.

Even what Thomas touched
in hands & side
was hollowness.

Moles

Little plush clots that undermine

arterial

& impulsive

plotting a black trajectory that seems

careless of detection

nimble as puppeteer's gloves,

I have to love them.

Tim says when he was a kid

men went for the skins:

flayed shadows of Peter Pan's

lost boys. Earth-turning,

ground shudder.

Other in every way, they tunnel on

indifferent. I believe

without ever seeing.

LIFE HALVED & PARTED

Not till life halved, and parted
one from the other,
did time begin, and knowledge;
sorrow, delight.
Terror of being apart, being lost
made real the night ...

– JUDITH WRIGHT,
'In Praise of Marriages'

Transatlantic

It's hard to accept that your day there
rolls on, is still to happen
while mine is done

as it's hard to accept that the dead
go on, loving, growing even
distinctly away from us,
their voices thinner than telephone wire.

What kind of letter can bridge this?
How can the feet we once
dropped all disgust to kiss step calmly
over new continents or turn firmly
for destinations unseen by us?

Dust is the mouth's taste
in absence, dust the ground
that swallows all footprints
with indifference.

Flight

For the moment you're so far gone my words
    can't reach you
and still be true. Invalid, fish
out of language, suspended,
water now just so much
expanse nobody uses. Twenty-four hours:
    only a day away,
resistant as tomorrow. This
my projection, fake Mercator, flattens the known
intractable, mere lines a poor
stand-in for presence, eruption, the very
    fluidity
that time and again defeats us where
we planned to annexe. I'm not
all states by any means, the world's contracted
    on microchips
that do but play us, and you out there
float free as a foetus
restating globally
                    intimate histories
                            tyrannies of distance.

Bonfire Night

1

Note I'm still writing
at the kitchen table
though there's a whole house
now

    just as I kept making
manoeuvring room
for a once-big belly even after
the baby was born

or again in the way
we always count
in mother-tongue
even when broken in
to a foreign one

Ought to fill
this useless space
expansive as gas

not shrink back, contract
with cold

2

With absence, space collapses
& balloons, the body

loses edges
bleeds like letters
porous, vegetable

broods, tuberous
& indented where
it grew against stones

deformed but
warm under a
slipping sun

3

She calls it *bomb-fire*
doesn't like
the pyrotechnics

They burst my heart

holds my hand tight
as if I might float off like those
balloons, like ash

autumn on Midsummer Common
the night's a bright commercial
sponsored by shopping centres
flashing across the crowdface
which isn't yours

but the heart's hardy
as some old inner tube
patched & adequate
to get us home

the voice of loss
calls after itself
by megaphone
child seeking parent
name seeking name

Solstice

1

Now trees are mere
stains on grey linen
held up to the eye
that can't see you anyway

denying horizon or any sense
of progress, except
where fog clots to droplets
on weedy branches
as I approach
the empty house.

2

Midday & all's clear –
small window
into day, a mood lifting
before redescending.
Bare limbs clutch mistletoe
like cold comfort,
loving even the parasite.
Between white blind
& inky closure
each act of necessity
pared back, I condense
for your benefit.

3

And the refusal of stars
moon or any secondary
glimmer, under a thick
layer of yet more moisture
confirms the prospect
while obscuring it.
Night hives us who
can't hibernate, time
& distance outpace us.

Penelope's Chore

Trimming pilled bits of fluff
from a loved garment, I read
of Mary Wollstonecraft & her
indignance at the *supposed severance*
of virtue and intellect in women.
It's a dull task such as nuns
are given to occupy fingers at
recreation lest the devil
make work. Or, taking a more
noble view of it, to keep the mind
free for the things of God, & not
these upstart ideas. I could kid
myself it's creative – something magical
after all, in a makeover – say:
I'm restoring a work of art, even if
it's a cheap knit from the sports section
of a department store. Or see it as
negative stitching, paring the hairy
layers off to unleash a true self
which won't need trimming again till after
the next wash.

Reconstructing

(for my grandmother)

Not even standing now, your mint-green house –
A fire, I heard, but never discovered
The cause. I imagine spontaneous
Combustion, some internal timer set
Years before, unknowing, in banked rage.
Or did you will the spark from where you are
Wherever that is. Yes, I did go looking –
Your last address a simple name and date
Added beneath your mother's, two collapsed
Into the very pose you started with.
Strange gestation. *Richer dust concealed.*
Harder to guess your English-garden green
And peaty earth now secreted in ash.
I come here too, pilgrim unbeliever
Pacing the street for where it must have been,
Surely – the thirsty lawn, the blank ghost gum
We children picked cicada casings from
Careful to keep intact; the Cape Lilac
Spreading its nasty carpet, poison ooze
Under the wheels as Mum and Dad drove off
Smiling through teeth. I never liked to leave.
You stood and waved until we disappeared.
Later I learned your small informal will
Left us that house 'if ever he should leave
Her with the children'. Saw that burnout coming,
But they did not, and shrugged bemusedly.
Your house was sold, the profit divided
For all the aunts and uncles, three good years
Before the final rift. If we had lived
In those too-few rooms that were all you had
Would fire have come the same and gutted us?

Touching the Iris

Halfway down Madingley Road the child
stops sobbing and plots your welcome
home, restoring order,
fingertips tracing the inner feather
of the sensitive iris. Blanched hands
thrust into our pathway, these plants
will wince and shrivel quickly, like bluebell,
like Lent-lily, shortlived
as butterfly wings, each stage
in Cambridge gardens planned
to cover the last one's end,
managing absence
with legerdemain. But she's oblivious
to cycles, seasons, merely sees
tight buds as promise, long sheaths
wound like streamers that might
at any moment shoot.

The Separation

Coarse as blotters, the sheets
resist her solo efforts
to square them.

Loose ghosts that won't
be broken in,
they haunt with faint
stains despite laundering.

However she wrestles,
they bulk out
like sails but sink,
directionless.
No one to catch the end
like wind,
no one to match her.

All in a heap they try
shrouding the furniture
as they tried to spread that
absence in the bed.

Like letters she shouldn't have read
they will not be
re-folded.

Rain

(for Michael)

'Mine, O thou lord of life, send my roots rain'
— GERARD MANLEY HOPKINS

1

You drive as the rain drives
now steady   now squalling
a car full of storm and vespers

One voice in the mass
seeks you out and pierces
like those cruel frequencies
dogs keen at
unfelt by the rest of us

Another dimension, your pain,
the banks and brakes, the chervil
and the birds – the rain, even
invested and utterly private

Just for this moment I cross
into it, hurtling down
the relentless lane

2

To master hurt by sipping at it
to acquire the taste
or burn the lips senseless

Conversely to spit it out
like words a stroke wrote off
resurfacing

3

Stepping out
real rain can't touch you

Drought of another order
I have been there   forgotten
Tell me again

It's a kind of home
you're guiding us through
we may miss some allusions but
will stick with you

PARTIAL VISIONS

The Test

1

Lamp-wise, he shows me
lightning forked
in my eye
sudden, like knowing
at once my own limits:

sight thrown backward.

Little by little my grip
on the outside,
it seems, is giving up.

He will keep
tightening it
by refinement,
as long as I ask

but cannot stop the slide
to what – darkness?

I think not: a viscous
flood at the windows,
daylight gone private,
the life indoors.

2

Generous, I can be
while waiting
for lenses

naked of face, uncertain
of my own expression,
oblivious

of yours.
Bus for once
arrives on time,

even without my reading
the furry screen;
rain or otherwise, path

is fluid, weather's inside
the head. Estimate
point of descent & tread

the way only abandoned
feet know. Later today,
back to the old sharp-honed

assumptions, certainties
made to measure,
errors of nothing but judgement.

Union

ekleipsis – Greek: a forsaking

slow & silent yet fiercer now
than at any other moment
these bodies enact their
mutual abandonment
that power might
be gained by ceding power

when we think of eclipse
we picture them
fixed like that but
the image is provisional
they slide apart

this is the symbol
of their very difference
the medusa-face
we cannot bear except
by way of mirrors

averting the gaze
we approach each other
never more distant
more opposite
than in this union

Eclipse, Kenwick, 1974

It descended one schoolday
when we were children,
this darkness, the one condition
that enabled seeing
the element we turned in
yet allowed only partial vision:
bright ring, emblem of burning
bush and stark completion
slow-motion moon imposing
'O-gape of complete despair'
which is there, which is always
there; how we cherished
our little images,
pin-hole and television –
ersatz knowledges –
unaware you'd swallow year after
year after year and the one of us
who said, 'I am not afraid
to die because then I will see
the stars as I've always wanted.'
I have never forgotten
how still it was,
how the animals took on oddly
the same way they did
one summer, the day he died;
uneasy calm before that dry
and silent storm.
How we ate, drank and were merry
instead of lessons, and the teachers
told stories and pulled down the blinds.

Lunar Eclipse

'I shall be useful when I lie down finally'
— SYLVIA PLATH

When we were young we'd lie outside at night
because the heat drove us from beds sweat-soaked
as if life were leached & condensed from us
while we tried to sleep, even sheets too dense
for the body's escape. Flat on our backs
in buffalo grass & sand we imagined
the truth: we lay upright on a planet
facing other planets hung in the vast
blackness – not horizontal under sky
but part of it. All footholds slippery,
grounding provisional, the earth was then
a vehicle over whose actual course
we'd no control, we had to travel blind.
One night we felt ourselves obliterate
even the mirrored light the moon allowed,
our backs turned on the sun in what was like
an endless moment, but would soon be gone.
Now that I'm older I no longer sleep
outdoors, but know whenever I lie down
the walking world's a travesty & what
seems big in it is barely there at all.

Potatoes

Why eyes when these are fingers,
wriggling out, obscene,
revealed in the low closet
by my child, seeking treasures.
Uprooted from any element,
they roll and wobble – too small
or odd for any meal,
passed over yet not tossed out,
despite reminders,
broodily shooting purple feelers, flesh
sagged as the back of my father's hands
digging and pressing.
Later I watched him
tugging the stems gone dry
a whole plant spent for its
coveted roots, this nest of eggs
plundered by little accomplices.
Now I am looking for good ones
to feed us, scrubbing & gouging
till half the substance is gone.

Peahen, University of Western Australia

1

Preening tail feathers, her head
and neck bend around
as if merely another appendage

yet for all her
Diplodocus-bulk, the bird
cannot be said to waddle

her disproportion more like
that of a fashion model, feet
turned out, self-consciously

symbolic, the School
of Arts overstating
its case.

2

Absurdly sprouting head
neck that lurches as if
head would somersault
away from body

massive horizontal weight
she surely can't support
on such lame props

all question grace, the whole
insistently beautiful, despite
her lack of tail.

3

She leads her chicks in & out of
these would-be cloisters

white as bride or ghost as if
by whiteness only she can
outstrip her mate

the gates are open but
she never goes out.

Peacock, Minnivale

Back on the farm
we visited as kids
there was always one peacock

flashing his excess
where all was pragmatic.

Parading for no one,
he kept aloof
from those meaner creatures
destined for table.

I liked his facile
complacency
being a city cousin
neither pretty nor suited
to the kitchen –
I imagined him as
I imagined freedom.

Yet now you tell me
there's one on every farm
merely for frightening foxes

kept not for aesthetics but
for the raw, half-strangled voice.

Sand

Where little bits of us got lost forever –
mystery never resolved, how it could wholly
swallow a marble or matchbox car.
We'd bore small tunnels that always collapsed
though shored hard, arms furred with crystals
as we pulled out. We'd heard of cave-ins that
filled bodily holes with golden amalgam,
dry drowning. So solid, yet shifting
like those grains in the wheat bin that
also terrified, seed reclaiming flesh
for clay. And the way it could
sting you to blindness if pitched
even in innocence, warm antipodean
version of the snowball, covering all.

Snow

If coldness here then only
something fully-fledged
   that scuffled
      in the courtyard
& survived
left this upheaval
in every direction

Something that got loose
   just in time
      before central heating
      & hot-water system
      admitted their failings
before the house
   gave in

Something I sensed
   coming, though not
      born to it
in the complete cessation
      of movement
      in the sky's tightness

Something intact
   The level of shutdown
   The going on

Of Frost & Shadow

Frost sticks with shadow till the liquid end
Because opposites are not
All that attracts, & like
May marry like, however hapless
Spreading itself broad & thin but
Narrowing down to flat silhouettes
Of house, of tree
    To a ghost of itself
    To its true home
As sun wears on.
Only the dark parts cleave
To their negative, their stencilled
Identity –
Night's forms flung prostrate
Like Pompeii's found objects
    Curved dog
    Woman fleeing
Essence of frost & shadow also
Slips its cast
When time is out.

The Translation

(for Françoise Hàn)

1

Barbarous –
they don't make them
like this
where I come from

mute & resistant as
locked concertinas

tricky as origami.

Why so nervous?
Hymeneal comparisons
are obvious
but odious.

I try with scissors
then kitchen knife –
too coarse

like skinning potatoes
with a dulled blade

how to get in there
without risking substance?

All right, I tell myself, I'll
only cut the ones I really need
to read

but a little success
makes me ruthless
soon I am plundering
whole sections
filleting blanks & endpapers

slicing them off like bandages
after cataracts
until at last the text
is open.

2

Are you sure you want to
go through with this?

Close as marriage but perhaps
without the benefits

sharing your word-house with
a stranger who keeps moving

the furniture, or worse
rips up floorboards to feed

the fireplace.

3

Chess-by-numbers where it's always
my turn, & I must second-guess
your every move.

4

I hedge along pages
like someone dipping
a toe at the pool's edge
or is it an ocean?

Better to plunge in
& be done with
notions of safety,
autonomy, I am already

in up to my neck
& staying afloat
is the same act
whatever the depth.

5

Traduire, c'est trahir
but the pun gives up its rhyme in
my language. At school they told us
poetry doesn't translate
in the same way
we'd learnt you couldn't
take large numbers from small ones –
only part of the picture. If they'd admitted
nothing translates & therefore
everything does, we might have
lost faith altogether.
Or stayed there, bipartisan,
in the between-zone, trusting entirely
the point of zero.

6

Only the capacity to love
   otherness
can bring us there
   finally

always the temptation
to present
   my version
      or fawn
   to yours

an act of balance
   a lens
less than perfect but
   accommodating
loving the way the eye
   loves light
but may also be
   destroyed by it

keeping open.